spot

HOLIDAYS

EASTER

D1300508

by Mari Schuh

AMICUS | AMICUS INK

cross

lily

Look for these words and pictures as you read.

eggs

basket

It is spring!
Easter will be here soon.

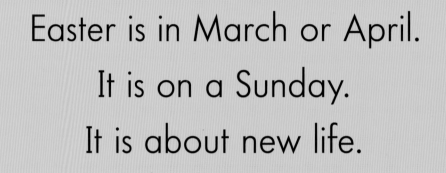

Easter is in March or April.

It is on a Sunday.

It is about new life.

cross

See the cross?

It is a Christian symbol.

Easter celebrates

Jesus' new life.

See the lily?
It is a flower.
It is a sign of hope.

lily

See the eggs?
Hard-boiled eggs are painted.
They are hidden. Kids find them.

eggs

See the basket?
It is full of treats.
Yum!

basket

Families get together.
They have a happy Easter!

cross

lily

Did you find?

eggs

basket

Spot is published by Amicus and Amicus Ink
P.O. Box 1329, Mankato, MN 56002
www.amicuspublishing.us

Library of Congress Cataloging-in-Publication Data
Names: Schuh, Mari C., 1975- author.
Title: Easter / by Mari Schuh.
Description: Mankato, Minnesota : Amicus, 2020. | Series:
  Spot holidays
Identifiers: LCCN 2018047358 (print) | LCCN 2019013572
  (ebook) | ISBN 9781681518435 (pdf) | ISBN
  9781681518039 (library binding) | ISBN
  9781681525310 (pbk.)
Subjects: LCSH: Easter--Juvenile literature. | CYAC:
  Easter. | Holidays.
Classification: LCC GT4935 (ebook) | LCC GT4935 .S345
  2020 (print) | DDC 394.2667--dc23
LC record available at https://lccn.loc.gov/2018047358

Printed in China

HC 10 9 8 7 6 5 4 3 2 1
PB 10 9 8 7 6 5 4 3 2 1

Alissa Thielges, editor
Deb Miner, series designer
Veronica Scott, book designer
Holly Young and Shane Freed,
  photo researchers

Photos by Shutterstock/Lora Liu, cover,
16; Shutterstock/Ivonne Wierink
1; Shutterstock/Darren Baker 3;
Getty/RomoloTavani 4–5; Getty/
Westend61 6–7; Getty/duckycards
8–9; Shutterstock/Billion Photos
10–11; Getty/Bluemoon Stock 12–13;
Shutterstock/LightField Studios 14–15

EASTER